First Star

The Blue-Pillowed Sky

A Shiny Golden Path

Rainbow Bridge

Slide Down the Sky

From Sea to Shining Sea

Time for Dreams

Across the World

Over the Moon

Sound of the Sea

Promises to Keep

Sometimes I think how lovely a garden
    would be
A garden in a cloud,
With raindrop flowers shining, snowflake
    blossoms drifting,
And a tree with spreading frost leaves
A rainbow bridge across a stream,
And cotton-wool grass which is softer
    than any earthly grass.
It must be beautiful to dance there.

—Carol Webb, Age 9

Rainbow Bridge

An anthology
compiled and edited by

Betty Modaressi and **Jan Hirshberg**

Program Authors

Jan Hirshberg
Ann Hughes
S.A. Bernier
Nellie Thomas
Carl Bereiter
Valerie Anderson
Jerome D. Lebo

Open Court
La Salle, Illinois

President and Publisher
M. Blouke Carus

Education Director
Carl Bereiter

Project Coordination
Marsha Roit

Project Planning and Implementation
Thomas G. Anderson,
Commonwealth Strategies, Inc.

Senior Editor
Marilyn Cunningham

Permissions
Diane Sikora

Art Direction
Todd Sanders

Cover Design
James Buddenbaum

OPEN COURT and ✿ are registered in the
U. S. Patent and Trademark Office.

Printed in the United States of America

ISBN 0-8126-1315-5

Acknowledgments

Grateful acknowledgment is given to the following publishers and copyright owners for permission granted to reprint selections from their publications. All possible care has been taken to trace ownership and secure permission for each selection included.

Addison-Wesley Publishing Company, Inc., for "I Am Rose" by Gertrude Stein, from *The World Is Round*; © 1966 Addison-Wesley Publishing Company, Inc., Reading, Massachusetts.

E. P. Dutton, a division of NAL Penguin Inc., for *Clyde Monster* by Robert L. Crowe; text copyright © 1976 by Robert L. Crowe.

Harper & Row, Publishers, Inc., for abridgement of complete text and ten illustrations from *My Hands*, written and illustrated by Aliki (Thomas Y. Crowell); copyright © 1962 by Aliki Brandenberg.

Harper & Row, Publishers, Inc., and William Heinemann Limited: for text and art of "Goblin Story," from *Little Bear's Visit*, written by Else Holmelund Minarik, illustrated by Maurice Sendak, text copyright © 1961 by Else Holmelund Minarik, pictures copyright © 1961 by Maurice Sendak; and for text and four illustrations from "Strange Bumps," from *Owl at Home*, written and illustrated by Arnold Lobel, copyright © 1975 by Arnold Lobel.

A. M. Heath & Company Limited, Authors' Agents, for "Little Green Riding Hood," from *Telephone Tales* by Gianni Rodari.

Macmillan Publishing Company: for "The Little Turtle," from *Collected Poems* by Vachel Lindsay, copyright 1920 by Macmillan Publishing Company, renewed 1948 by Elizabeth C. Lindsay; and for *Willaby* by Rachel Isadora, copyright © 1977 by Rachel Isadora.

Macmillan Publishing Company and William Heinemann Limited, for "Abu Ali Counts His Donkeys," from *Abu Ali: Three Tales of the Middle East* by Dorothy O. Van Woerkom; text copyright © 1976 by Dorothy O. Van Woerkom.

G. P. Putnam's Sons, for "When I Was Lost" by Dorothy Aldis from *All Together* by Dorothy Aldis: copyright 1925–1928, 1934, 1939, 1952; copyright renewed 1953–1956, 1962, 1967 by Dorothy Aldis.

Simon & Schuster, Inc., for the poem on page ii ("An Enchanted Garden") by Carol Webb, from *Miracles*; copyright © 1966 by Richard Lewis.

Illustration

Aliki (96–101), Victor Ambrus (14–22), Bill and Judie Anderson (68–76), Cheryl Arnemann (59), Lois Axeman (45), Pam Carroll (102), Gwen Connelly (7–9, 108–112), David Cunningham (3–5, 116–121), Tom Dunnington (23–24), Andrea Eberbach (114–115), Lois Ehlert (67–78), Mark Frueh (cover), Michael Hague (1–3, 65–66, 77, 82–83), Marika Hahn (10–11), Dennis Hockerman (113), Ann Iosa (122–125), Rachel Isadora (61–64), Arnold Lobel (92–95), Walter Lorraine (103–107), Diana Magnuson (55, 57, 58), Dick Martin (49–54, 126–131), Sharron O'Neill (46–48), Suzanne Richardson (60), Maurice Sendak (25–36), Roz Schanzer (38–44), Steven Schiendler (25–36), Dan Siculan (79–81), Jan Wills (85–91)

Contents

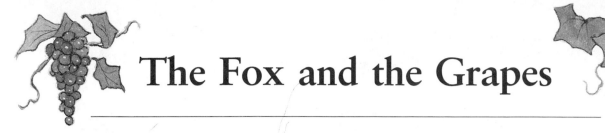

The Fox and the Grapes

AESOP

One day a fox was running down a dusty road. He was hot and thirsty. Soon he saw some grapes hanging on a vine in a garden nearby.

The grapes were large and ripe and juicy. They seemed quite tasty to the hot, thirsty fox.

"How I wish I had some of those grapes," said the fox.

The fox jumped high in the air and reached up with his paw, but he did not get the grapes.

He jumped higher and higher, but he still was not able to get the grapes.

At last the fox had to give up.

"Those grapes can stay on the vine," said the fox with a yawn. "I can tell that they are sour, and they must taste awful. I don't like sour grapes."

Gran's Auto

ELIZABETH LANGENDOERFER

"Here I am, Gran," said Paula. "Why did you ask me to come to your house?"

"I asked you to come because I'm going to take you for a ride in my new auto," said Gran.

Gran opened the garage. Inside was a fantastic, old car. Gran patted its tail fin and said, "How do you like it, Paula? I just got it yesterday. Isn't it the finest auto you've ever seen?"

"Well," said Paula, pausing. "It is a car, but it's not new. Why did you get this old car? You can't even drive."

"I can so drive," said Gran. "I've taken driving lessons for six weeks. I have my driver's license. My teacher said that I'm ready to drive by myself now, so I got a car. It's just like the one I liked so much about thirty years ago."

"The old car is pretty," said Paula, "but you really don't need to drive. Mom and Dad drive you where you need to go. Lots of people take you places."

"I don't like to wait for people to take me where I need to go," said Gran. "Your mom and dad won't have to haul my groceries home from the market every week. They won't have to pick up my laundry. I can do things myself. I can be on my own."

5

Gran and Paula got into the car. "Buckle your seat belt," said Gran. "I had to get new ones for my auto. It didn't have seat belts when I got it."

Gran turned the key, and the old car started right up. She backed out of the garage, and soon they were heading down the highway.

Gran and Paula were quite a sight in the old car. Every place they went, people stared at them and smiled. The old car ran just as it had when it was new.

When they got back to Gran's house, Paula said, "This is a grand, old car, Gran. I'm glad you got it. May we go for more rides in it?"

"We may go whenever you feel like it," said Gran, "but remember one thing. This isn't just an old car. It's my auto."

Early Automobiles

B. ADKINS

People have been going from place to place in automobiles for many years. In the late 1800s automobiles were new and strange. Most people had to go to circuses to see the strange cars.

Early automobiles were powered by steam engines. To make the steam that powered the engines, water was heated over open fires. Many times people riding in the steam-powered automobiles were burned by the fire or by the steam.

People wanted safer automobiles. Soon electric automobiles were invented. Electric automobiles were powered by batteries. People liked electric automobiles. They were easy to drive. They ran quietly, and they were safe.

Electric automobiles did not run fast, and their batteries had to be recharged about every fifty miles.

People wanted automobiles they could use for trips. Automobiles with gasoline-powered engines replaced steam-powered and electric automobiles.

In the early 1900s gasoline was cheap. People could drive gasoline-powered automobiles for many miles. In those days each piece of an automobile had to be handmade. The pieces then had to be fitted together by hand. Not many automobiles were made, and not many people could own them.

The House That Jack Built

MOTHER GOOSE

This is the house
That Jack built.
This is the malt
That lay in the house that Jack built.

This is the rat,
That ate the malt
That lay in the house that Jack built.

This is the cat,

That killed the rat,

That ate the malt

That lay in the house that Jack built.

This is the dog,

That bothered the cat,

That killed the rat,

That ate the malt

That lay in the house that Jack built.

This is the cow with the crumpled horn,

That tossed the dog,

That bothered the cat,

That killed the rat,

That ate the malt

That lay in the house that Jack built.

This is the maiden all forlorn,

That milked the cow with the crumpled horn,

That tossed the dog,

That bothered the cat,

That killed the rat,

That ate the malt

That lay in the house that Jack built.

12

This is the man all tattered and torn,

That kissed the maiden all forlorn,

That milked the cow with the crumpled horn,

That tossed the dog,

That bothered the cat,

That killed the rat,

That ate the malt

That lay in the house that Jack built.

The Three Bears

ROBERT SOUTHEY

[PART 1]

Once upon a time there were three bears—a great, big bear, a middle-sized bear, and a little, tiny bear. They all lived together in a house in the middle of a forest.

One day the three bears sat down to breakfast. Their porridge was too hot to eat. They decided to go for a walk and leave the porridge on the kitchen table to cool off.

While they were away, a little girl named Goldilocks came to the house in the forest. She had been picking flowers since early in the morning and was very tired. When she saw the little house, she said to herself, "The people who live here might let me rest for a while."

She rapped on the door, but nobody came because the three bears were out walking in the forest. She rapped again, and still nobody came. Then Goldilocks opened the door and walked right in.

The first things she saw were three bowls of porridge on the kitchen table. Goldilocks was hungry, so she started to eat the great, big bowl of porridge.

"This is too hot!" she said to herself.

Then she took a taste from the middle-sized bowl. "This is too cold!" she said to herself.

Then she took a taste from the little, tiny bowl. "This is just right!" she said to herself, and she ate it all up.

Then Goldilocks went into the living room to rest for a while, and there she saw three chairs near the fireplace.

First she sat down in the great, big chair.
"This is too high!" she said to herself.

Then she sat down on the middle-sized chair.
"This is too wide!" she said to herself.

Then she sat down in the little, tiny chair.
"This is just right!" she exclaimed, and she sat
down so hard that the little, tiny chair broke into
a hundred pieces.

[PART 2]

After Goldilocks broke the little, tiny chair, she went upstairs. There she saw three beds standing in a row. First she lay down on the great, big bed. "This is too hard!" she said to herself.

Then she lay down on the middle-sized bed. "This is too soft!" she said to herself.

Then she lay down on the little, tiny bed. "This is just right!" she said to herself, and she fell fast asleep.

After a while the three bears came home from their walk in the forest. They were very hungry now and started to eat their porridge.

The great, big bear took one taste from his bowl and growled, "SOMEONE HAS BEEN EATING MY PORRIDGE!"

The middle-sized bear took one taste from her bowl and said, "Someone has been eating my porridge!"

The little, tiny bear squeaked, *"Someone has been eating my porridge and has eaten it all up!"*

Then the three bears went into the living room.

"SOMEONE HAS BEEN SITTING IN MY CHAIR!" growled the great, big bear.

"SOMEONE HAS BEEN SITTING IN MY CHAIR!" said the middle-sized bear.

"*Someone has been sitting in my chair,*" squeaked the little, tiny bear, "*and has broken it all to pieces!*"

Then the three bears went upstairs.

"SOMEONE HAS BEEN SLEEPING IN MY BED!" growled the great, big bear.

"SOMEONE HAS BEEN SLEEPING IN MY BED!" said the middle-sized bear.

"*Someone has been sleeping in my bed,*" squeaked the little, tiny bear, "*and here she is!*"

Goldilocks heard the little, tiny bear and woke up. When she saw the three bears, she was so frightened that she jumped out of bed, bounded down the stairs, and ran all the way home to her mother. She never went back to the house of the three bears again.

The Lion and the Mouse

AESOP

One day a little mouse accidentally ran across the paws of a sleeping lion. This woke the lion up, and he became very angry. He grabbed the mouse with his huge paw and opened his mouth to swallow her. Just then the mouse cried out, "Please, kind sir, I didn't mean to wake you up. If you let me go now, I will help you some day."

The lion thought the idea of a mouse helping a lion was so funny that he let the mouse go free.

A week later the lion was caught in a
hunter's net. The little mouse heard him roaring
and went closer to see what the trouble was.
When she saw that the lion was in the trap, she
remembered her promise and began to gnaw the
rope. She kept gnawing and gnawing until soon
the mighty king of beasts was free.

"You see?" asked the mouse. "Wasn't I right
about helping you?"

And so the lion learned that even little
friends can be great friends.

Goblin Story

A FAIRY TALE
ELSE HOLMELUND MINARIK

[PART 1]

One day a little goblin
went by an old cave.
It was old,
it was cold,
it was dark.

And something inside it went bump.

What was that?

BUMP!

"Hoo-ooh—" cried the goblin.

He got so scared that he jumped
right out of his shoes.
Then he began to run.

Pit-pat-pit-pat-pit-pat———

What was that?

SOMETHING was running after him.

Oh my goodness, what could it be?

The goblin was too scared to look back.

He ran faster than ever.

But so did the SOMETHING that went

pit-pat-pit-pat-pit-pat———

The goblin saw a hole in a tree.

He jumped inside to hide.

The pit-pat-pit-pat came closer,

closer—CLOSER—till it stopped,

right by the hole in the tree!

[PART 2]

Then all was quiet.

Nothing happened.

Nothing.

The little goblin wanted to peek out.

It was so quiet.

Should he peek out?

Yes, he would. He WOULD peek out!

And he did.

"Eeeeeh———!" cried the goblin.

Do you know what he saw?

He saw—his SHOES!
His own little shoes
—and nothing more.
"Goodness," said the goblin,
hopping out of the tree.

"That old bump in the cave
made me jump right out of my shoes.
But they came running after me,
didn't they!
And here they are!"

He picked up his shoes,
hugged them,
and put them back on.

"Good little shoes," said the goblin.
"You didn't want to stay behind,
did you!" He laughed.

"Who cares about an old bump,
anyway," he said.
So he snapped his fingers,
and skipped away—just like that!

The Little Engine That Could

AUTHOR UNKNOWN

[PART 1]

A little steam engine had a long train of cars to pull.

She went along very well till she came to a steep hill. Then, no matter how hard she tried, she could not move the long train of cars.

She pulled and pulled. She puffed and puffed. She backed up and started off again. Choo! Choo!

But no! The cars would not go up the hill.

At last she left the train and started up the track alone. Do you think she had stopped working? No, indeed! She was going for help.

"Surely I can find someone to help me," she thought.

Over the hill and up the track went the little steam engine. Choo, choo! Choo, choo! Choo, choo!

Pretty soon the little steam engine saw a big steam engine standing on a sidetrack, looking very big and strong. Running alongside, she looked up and said, "Will you help me over the hill with my train of cars? It is so long and heavy that I can't pull it over."

The big steam engine looked down at the little steam engine. Then she said, "Don't you see that I have finished my day's work? I have been rubbed and scoured, ready for my next run. No, I cannot help you."

[PART 2]

The little steam engine was sorry, but she went on. Choo, choo! Choo, choo! Choo, choo! Soon she came to a second big steam engine standing on a sidetrack. He was puffing and puffing, as if he were tired.

"He may help me," thought the little steam engine. She ran alongside and asked, "Will you help me bring my train of cars over the hill? It is so long and so heavy that I can't get it over."

The second big steam engine answered, "I have just come in from a long, long run. Don't you see how tired I am? Can't you get some other engine to help you this time?"

"I'll try," said the little steam engine, and off she went. Choo, choo! Choo, choo! Choo, choo!

After a while she came to a little steam engine just like herself. She ran alongside and said, "Will you help me over the hill with my train of cars? It is so long and so heavy that I can't pull it over."

"Yes, indeed!" said this little steam engine. "I'll be glad to help you, if I can."

So the two little steam engines started back to where the train of cars had been standing. Both little steam engines went to the head of the train, one behind the other.

Puff, puff! Chug, choo! Off they started!

Slowly the cars began to move. Slowly they climbed the steep hill. As they climbed, each little steam engine began to sing,

"I—think—I—can! I—think—I—can!

I—think—I—can! I—think—I—can!

I—think—I—can! I—think—I—can!

I—think—I—can! I—think—I—can!

I—think—I—can! I—think—I—can!"

And they did! Very soon they were over the hill and going down the other side.

43

Now they were on the plain again, and the little steam engine could pull her train herself. She thanked the little engine who had come to help her and said good-by.

And she went merrily on her way, singing, "I-thought-I-could! I-thought-I-could! I-thought-I-could! I-thought-I-could! I-thought-I-could! I-thought-I-could! I-thought-I-could! I-thought-I-could! I-thought-I-could! I-thought-I-could! I-thought-I-could!"

Betty Botter

ANONYMOUS

Betty Botter bought some butter,
"But," she said, "the butter's bitter;
If I put it in my batter,
It will make by batter bitter;
But a bit of better butter—
That—would make my batter better."
So she bought a bit of butter,
Better than her bitter butter,
And she put it in her batter,
And the batter was not bitter.
So 'twas better Betty Botter
Bought a bit of better butter.

The Hare and the Tortoise

AESOP

One time a hare said to some animals, "No one can beat me in a race. I can run like the wind. Who will dare to race with me?"

All of the animals were silent because they were afraid to race with the hare.

At last the tortoise said quietly, "The claims you make sound phony to me. You can't win every race. No one can really run as fast as the wind blows. I will run a race with you."

"That's a joke," said the hare with a sly grin. "I will be out of sight before you get started."

"Wait until you have won the race before you make more phony claims," said the tortoise. "Shall we race?"

The hare agreed. They decided to start the race at a nearby tree. They'd race down the lane and across the bridge. Then they'd turn around and race back to the tree.

The race began. Soon the hare was far ahead of the tortoise.

The hare had run so fast that she soon became tired. When she got to the bridge, she sat down and leaned against it to rest. She was sure she had time to take a nap and still win the race.

The tortoise plodded slowly down the lane. He crossed the bridge and started back up the lane.

When the hare woke up, the tortoise had almost reached the tree.

The hare jumped up and ran across the bridge. Then she raced up the lane. But she was not in time. The tortoise reached the tree first and won the race.

The animals cheered and gave the tortoise a big trophy.

The tortoise turned to the animals and said, "I found out long ago that if you do something steadily, you can do it well most of the time, even if you are slow."

The Three Billy Goats Gruff

A NORSE FOLK TALE

[PART 1]

Once upon a time there were three billy goats named Gruff. They were all going up to the hillside to eat the moist grass that grew in the rich soil there. They wanted to make themselves fat.

On the way to the hillside they had to cross an old, wooden bridge. In the bushes under the bridge lived a huge, ugly troll. His eyes were as big as saucers, and his nose was as long as a poker.

The smallest billy goat Gruff crossed the bridge first. "Trip, trap! Trip, trap!" went his little feet on the bridge.

The troll stamped his foot and roared in his mean voice, "Who's that tripping over my bridge?"

"It is only I, the little billy goat Gruff," said the billy goat with his small voice.

"I'm coming to gobble you up," shouted the troll.

"You don't want to eat me. I'm too little," said the small billy goat with his little voice. "Wait until the next billy goat Gruff comes. He's much bigger."

"All right. Be off with you, then," said the troll.

A little while later, the middle-sized billy goat Gruff started across the bridge.

"TRIP, TRAP! TRIP, TRAP! TRIP, TRAP!" went the middle-sized billy goat's feet on the bridge.

"Who's that tripping over my bridge?" roared the troll in a meaner voice.

"It is I, the middle-sized billy goat Gruff. I'm going up to the hillside to make myself fat," said the middle-sized billy goat, who had a louder voice than his brother.

"I'm coming to gobble you up," said the troll.

"You don't want to eat me," said the billy goat. "Wait until the big billy goat Gruff comes. He's much bigger."

"All right. Be off with you, then," said the troll.

52

[PART 2]

Soon the big billy goat Gruff started across
the bridge.

"TRIP! TRAP! TRIP! TRAP! TRIP! TRAP!"
went the big billy goat's feet on the bridge. The
big billy goat was so heavy that the bridge
creaked and groaned under him.

The troll heard the noise on the bridge. He
was afraid that the bridge was being destroyed.

"Who's that tramping over my bridge?"
roared the troll in his meanest voice.

"IT IS I, BIG BILLY GOAT GRUFF!" said
the billy goat in his big voice. He put his head
down, and he flew at the troll. He hoisted the
troll up into the air and tossed him into the river.
After that the big billy goat Gruff went up to the
hillside to enjoy eating the grass. The billy goats
had a good time on the hillside. They ate until
they had had their fill. Soon they were so fat that
they were hardly able to walk home again.

Lost and Mixed Up

BETTY MODARESSI

Pedro sat in the big chair next to Officer Carmella for a long time. Pedro was lost. He was a little afraid, and he was very mixed up. In fact, he was so mixed up that he was not even able to remember his last name. Pedro felt awful.

"Think hard, Pedro," said Officer Carmella. "Do you know your telephone number?"

"I know it," said Pedro, "but I can't remember it."

"Can you tell me what street you live on?" asked Officer Carmella.

"I know I live on Grace Street," said Pedro. "I can't remember my house number."

While Pedro was trying to think of his telephone and house numbers, his last name popped into his mind. "My last name is Gomez," Pedro called out. "I finally remember it!"

"Now," said Officer Carmella. "We'll check the telephone book to find a Gomez family on Grace Street. Then we'll call your mom and dad and tell them you are here."

Officer Carmella scratched her head. "This isn't going to be easy," she said. "Three people named Gomez live on Grace Street. Tom Gomez lives at 189 West Grace Street. Ricardo Gomez lives at 43 West Grace Street. Elena Gomez lives at 82 East Grace Street. Now, let me see. Who will I call first?"

"That's easy," said Pedro. "All of those people are in my family. Tom is my dad, Ricardo is my uncle, and Elena is my grandma. You can call all of them."

"I'll call your dad first," said Officer Carmella. "He and your mom will want to know where you are."

Before Officer Carmella picked up the phone to dial the number she had found, two frightened people ran up to her.

"We're trying to find our little boy," the man shouted. "His name is Pedro Gomez. We're his mom and dad."

"You've come to the right place," said Officer Carmella. "He's right here. I was just getting ready to call you to tell you where he is."

Pedro ran to his mom and dad. They hugged and kissed. Then they all began talking at the same time.

Officer Carmella just smiled. She likes happy endings.

When I Was Lost

DOROTHY ALDIS

Underneath my belt
My stomach was a stone.
Sinking was the way I felt.
And hollow.
And alone.

I Am Rose

GERTRUDE STEIN

I am Rose my eyes are blue
I am Rose and who are you?
I am Rose and when I sing
I am Rose like anything.

Willaby

RACHEL ISADORA

Willaby is in first grade. She likes math, lunch, her teacher Miss Finney, and science. But best of all Willaby likes to draw.

When the other children are playing, Willaby is drawing. She draws on her desk when all the others write the history lesson in their notebooks.

At home Willaby sometimes uses up all her paper. Then she draws on the walls in her bedroom.

One Monday morning when Willaby goes to school, Miss Finney is not there. The substitute teacher, Mrs. Benjamin, tells the class that Miss Finney is sick and will not come back to school until the following Monday. The class decides to send Miss Finney get-well cards. They make up a poem, and Mrs. Benjamin writes it on the blackboard.

Soon everyone is busy copying the poem. Except for Willaby. She is busy drawing a fire truck she saw on her way to school.

Before long Mrs. Benjamin asks the class to hand in their cards. Willaby doesn't know what to do. She forgot all about the get-well card, and now there is no time to copy the poem.

The children put their cards in a big envelope.

On the way home from school, Willaby suddenly remembers she didn't sign her name on her card! Now Miss Finney will never know that she sent her a card. Miss Finney might think she doesn't like her.

During the week Willaby makes thirty-seven get-well cards for Miss Finney. She signs every one. But when Monday morning comes, Willaby does not feel like going to school. Instead of taking the bus, she decides to walk to school.

At school Willaby walks to her seat without looking at Miss Finney. But when she sits down at her desk . . .

Dear Willaby,
Thank you for the get-well picture.

Miss Finney

Willaby doesn't give Miss Finney the thirty-seven get-well cards. She doesn't have to!

The Wolf in Sheep's Clothing

AESOP

One day a wolf found a sheep's skin. He wrapped himself in it and sneaked into a sheep pen. He ate a lamb. He was sneaking up on a second lamb when the shepherd caught him.

"Don't throw me out," said the wolf. "I'm one of your sheep."

"You're only pretending to be a sheep," said the shepherd. "I'm no fool. I know you're really a wolf."

"How do you know?" asked the wolf. "I look like a sheep."

"You say you are a sheep, and you do look like a sheep," said the shepherd, "but you act like a wolf." The shepherd pulled a limb from a tree and beat the wolf with it. The wolf leaped the fence and climbed a nearby hill. He never went back to the sheep pen.

The Little Turtle

VACHEL LINDSAY

There was a little turtle.
He lived in a box.
He swam in a puddle.
He climbed on the rocks.

He snapped at a mosquito.
He snapped at a flea.
He snapped at a minnow,
And he snapped at me.

He caught the mosquito.
He caught the flea.
He caught the minnow.
But he didn't catch me.

The Gingerbread Boy

AN AMERICAN FOLK TALE

[PART 1]

Long ago there lived a little old woman and a little old man. They liked children and had always wanted children, but they had none.

One day the little old woman made a boy out of gingerbread. Before she put the gingerbread into the oven, she said, "I do wish you were a real boy. You could be the child we never had."

Then she put the gingerbread into the oven to bake.

After a while the little old woman opened the oven door to see whether the gingerbread was done.

Out jumped the Gingerbread Boy!

Away he ran, out the door and down the road. The little old woman and the little old man ran after him.

But the Gingerbread Boy looked back and called out,

Run! Run as fast as you can!

You can't catch me.

I'm the Gingerbread Man, I am! I am!

And they could not catch him.

The little Gingerbread Boy ran on and on.

Soon he came to a cow.

"Stop, little Gingerbread Boy,"
said the cow. "I should like to eat you."

But the little Gingerbread Boy called out,

I've run away from the little old woman,

I've run away from the little old man,

And I can run away from you,

I can! I can!

The cow ran after him.

But the Gingerbread Boy looked back
and called,

Run! Run as fast as you can!

You can't catch me.

I'm the Gingerbread Man, I am! I am!

And the cow could not catch him.

The little Gingerbread Boy ran on and on.

Soon he came to a horse.

"Please stop, little Gingerbread Boy," said
the horse. "You look good to eat. I would like to
eat you."

But the little Gingerbread Boy called out,
I've run away from a little old woman,
I've run away from a little old man,
I've run away from a cow,
And I can run away from you,
I can! I can!

The horse ran after him.

But the Gingerbread Boy looked back and called,

Run! Run as fast as you can!

You can't catch me.

I'm the Gingerbread Man, I am! I am!

And the horse could not catch him.

PART 2

By and by the Gingerbread Boy came to a farmer who was tending his corn.

The farmer saw the Gingerbread Boy and called, "Do not run so fast, little Gingerbread Boy. You look quite good to me. I would like to eat you."

But the little Gingerbread Boy ran faster and faster. As he ran, he called out,

I've run away from a little old woman,
I've run away from a little old man,
I've run away from a cow,
I've run away from a horse,
And I can run away from you,
I can! I can!

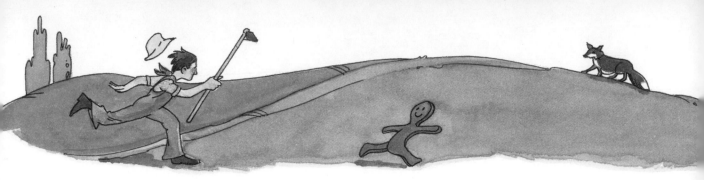

The farmer ran after him.

But the Gingerbread Boy looked back and called out,

Run! Run as fast as you can!

You can't catch me.

I'm the Gingerbread Man, I am! I am!

And the farmer could not catch him.

Then the little Gingerbread Boy met a fox.

By this time the little Gingerbread Boy was quite pleased with himself. He was pleased that he could run so fast, so he called out to the fox,

Run! Run as fast as you can!

You can't catch me.

I'm the Gingerbread Man, I am! I am!

I've run away from a little old woman,

I've run away from a little old man,

I've run away from a cow,

I've run away from a horse,

I've run away from a farmer,

And I can run away from you, I can! I can!

"Why," said the sly, old fox, "I wouldn't dream of trying to catch you."

Just then the little Gingerbread Boy came to a river. He dared not jump into the water. Still, the cow, the horse, and the people were chasing him, and he had to cross the river to keep out of their reach.

"Jump on my tail, and I will take you across the river," said the fox.

So the little Gingerbread Boy jumped on the fox's tail, and the fox swam into the river.

A small distance from shore the fox said, "Little Gingerbread Boy, I think you had better get on my back, or you may fall into the river!"

So the little Gingerbread Boy jumped onto the fox's back.

When they were in the middle of the river, the fox cried out suddenly, "The water is deep. You may get wet on my back. Jump up onto my nose!"

So the little Gingerbread Boy jumped up onto the fox's nose.

Then in a twinkling the fox threw back his head and —snip, snip, snap!—he ate up the Gingerbread Boy!

The Silkworm and the Spider

AESOP

One day a silkworm and a spider were working side by side. The silkworm was spinning silk slowly. The spider was spinning her web fast.

"See how quickly I spin," said the spider. "I spin much faster than you do. You must be the slowest worker in the world."

"Your words are true," said the silkworm. "I do work slowly, but I also work carefully. My work is worth more than yours is. People all over the world love my silk, but they brush your worthless cobwebs away."

The Spider

POET UNKNOWN

In the center of the web,
  The spider
Sat, waiting for a meal
  To tide her
Over to the end of day.

From the back of a chair
  He spied her
And a meal of a fly
  Denied her
When he quietly sneaked away.

The Plum Pit

LEO TOLSTOY

One day a father bought some plums at the store. He took the plums home, put them in a large bowl, and told his children not to eat them until after dinner. All of the children stood around the bowl and admired the special plums, but they did not eat them.

But little Johnny had never tasted plums
before. He had no notion of how they tasted.
When everyone had left the room, he took one of
the plums and ate it.

Before dinner Johnny's father saw that one of
the plums was gone. He told the children's
mother about it.

After dinner the children's mother said, "Did
any of you children eat one of these plums?"

All of the children said, "No." Johnny's face
turned as red as a beet, but he also said, "No, I
didn't eat it."

Then the mother said, "If one of you did eat a plum, that is bad, but that is not what worries me. What is worse is that plums have pits. If you eat the pit, it might choke you, and you might die."

Johnny turned pale and said, "No, I threw the pit out the window."

Then everyone laughed, and Johnny began to cry.

Finally the mother said, "Don't cry, Johnny. We know that you won't do anything like this again."

"No," said Johnny, "I won't. I promise."

The Elf and the Dormouse

OLIVER HERFORD

Under a toadstool
Crept a wee elf,
Out of the rain
To shelter himself.

Under the toadstool,
   Sound asleep,
Sat a big dormouse
   All in a heap.

Trembled the wee elf,
   Frightened, and yet
Fearing to fly away
   Lest he get wet.

To the next shelter—
   Maybe a mile!
Sudden the wee elf
   Smiled a wee smile.

Tugged till the toadstool
Toppled in two.
Holding it over him,
Gaily he flew.

Soon he was safe home,
Dry as could be.
Soon woke the dormouse—
"Good gracious me!

Where is my toadstool?"
Loud he lamented.
And that's how umbrellas
First were invented.

Jane Goodall

B. ADKINS

[PART 1]

A girl was watching a sea gull as it dived toward the water. The gull was looking for food. The girl counted the number of times the gull dived before it found food. She wrote a sentence about the gull in her notebook. Then she started walking home, watching for more birds as she went.

This girl, Jane Goodall, lived in England on the seacoast. She spent most of her time watching birds and animals. She watched robins, starlings, blackbirds, field mice, moles, and rabbits.

She wrote notes about the things they did. Jane wanted to learn how these birds and animals behaved. She spent her pocket money on books about animal behavior.

When Jane was eighteen, she left school to work in an office. She wanted to save money to go to Africa. After a time she had saved the money, and she was ready for the trip.

In Africa she met a noted scientist who was studying animal behavior too. His name was Dr. Louis Leakey. Jane became Dr. Leakey's helper and friend. Dr. Leakey knew that Jane did fine work with animals. He asked her to work on a special project on chimpanzees.

Jane went into the African forest and set up a camp near a large lake. She lived alone at a place where a group of chimpanzees lived. This way she would be able to watch them and learn how they behaved.

At first the chimpanzees ran away before
Jane could get close to them. They had never seen
a human being before. They were afraid of Jane.

Jane learned where the chimpanzees went to
eat in the morning. She would get up early and go
there before the chimps did. She sat quietly so
that the chimps would learn to know and trust
her. Slowly the chimpanzees lost their fear of Jane.

[PART 2]

During Jane's first year in the forest the chimps stopped running away when they saw her. Then they let her come as close as thirty feet. By the end of the second year they would come to Jane's camp.

People all over the world wanted to know more about Jane's work. She wrote articles about the chimpanzees and their ways of doing things. A film maker from Holland was so pleased with Jane's work that he made a movie about her and the chimps. Jane and the chimps were the main characters. The movie was shown on television.

Jane got pleasure from watching the chimps. When the chimps knew that Jane was their friend, she started her real work. She watched them as they played, worked, ate, and raised their young. She copied many of their ways and echoed their sounds. She spent a lot of time in the trees. She ate leaves, bananas, and even insects. She learned things about chimps that no one had known before.

Jane learned that chimps do not eat only leaves and fruit. They hunt for small animals to eat. She was the first to learn that chimpanzees make and use crude tools. Until Jane saw chimpanzees using sticks as tools, scientists had thought that human beings were the only living beings to make and use tools. Scientists treasure Jane's writings about the chimps. They say that Jane's discovery that chimps use tools is her most important discovery.

Strange Bumps

ARNOLD LOBEL

Owl was in bed. "It is time to blow out the candle and go to sleep," he said with a yawn. Then Owl saw two bumps under the blanket at the bottom of his bed. "What can those strange bumps be?" asked Owl.

Owl lifted up the blanket. He looked down into the bed. All he could see was darkness. Owl

tried to sleep, but he could not. "What if those two strange bumps grow bigger and bigger while I am asleep?" said Owl. "That would not be pleasant."

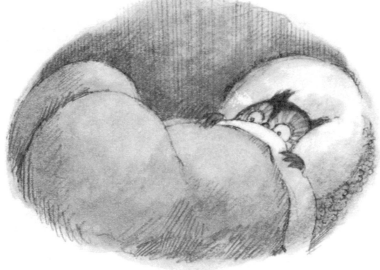

Owl moved his right foot up and down. The bump on the right moved up and down. "One of those bumps is moving!" said Owl.

Owl moved his left foot up and down. The bump on the left moved up and down. "The other bump is moving!" cried Owl.

Owl pulled all the covers off his bed. The bumps were gone. All Owl could see at the bottom of the bed were his own two feet. "But now I am cold," said Owl. "I will cover myself with the blankets again."

As soon as he did, he saw the same two bumps. "Those bumps are back!" shouted Owl. "Bumps, bumps, bumps! I will never sleep tonight!"

Owl jumped up and down on top of his bed. "Where are you? What are you?" he cried. With a crash and a bang the bed came falling down.

Owl ran down the stairs. He sat in his chair near the fire. "I will let those two strange bumps sit on my bed all by themselves," said Owl. "Let them grow as big as they wish. I will sleep right here where I am safe."

And that is what he did.

My Hands

ALIKI

I put my hands together. The fingers of my right hand touch the same fingers of my left hand.

Now I stretch my fingers. Two are different from all the others.

My thumbs! They point side to side when the others point up and down.

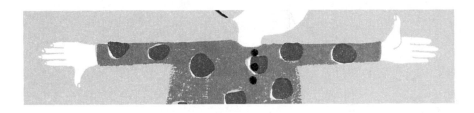

They point up and down when the others
point side to side.

My thumb can touch any
of my other fingers.

I use my thumb and fingers
to hold and grasp things.

Try to hold a pencil without using your thumb.

Try to button a button without using
your thumb.

It is not easy.

We use our thumbs all the time.

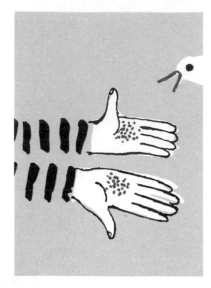

This is the palm of my hand.

I hold things in my palm.

I use my palms

to make snowballs.

I use my palms to roll clay.

These are my fingertips.

They tell me if I touch something

hot

cold

smooth

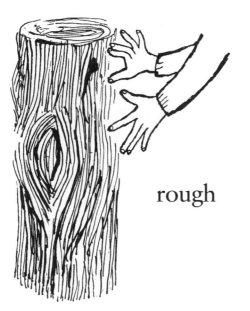

rough

or prickly.

Hands are different.
These are Daddy's hands.

These are Mother's hands . . .

. . . and Grandmother's hands.

These are baby sister's hands.

Her hands will grow to be as big as mine.

My hands will grow to be as big as Daddy's or Mother's.

But I can do many things with my hands right now.

I use my hands when I work hard.

The Itsy, Bitsy Spider

POET UNKNOWN

The itsy, bitsy spider

Climbed up the water spout.

Down came the rain

And washed the spider out.

Out came the sun

And dried up all the rain.

And the itsy, bitsy spider

climbed up the spout again.

Little Green Riding Hood

GIANNI RODARI

"Once upon a time there was a little girl called
Little Yellow Riding Hood."

"No! *Red* Riding Hood!"

"Oh yes, of course, Red Riding Hood.
Well, one day her mother called and said:
'Little Green Riding Hood————'"

"*Red!*"

"Sorry! Red. 'Now, my child, go to Aunt
Mary and take her these potatoes.'"

"No! It doesn't go like that! 'Go to Grandma
and take her these cakes.'"

"All right. So the little girl
went off, and in the wood she met
a giraffe."

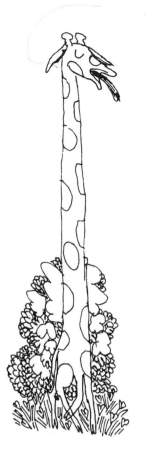

"What a mess you're making
of it! It was a wolf!"

"And the wolf said: 'What's six times eight?'"
"No! No! The wolf asked her where she
was going."

"So he did. And Little Black Riding Hood replied———"

"Red! Red!! Red!!!"

"She replied: 'I'm going to the market to buy some tomatoes.'"

"No, she didn't. She said: 'I'm going to my grandma, who is sick, but I've lost my way.'"

"Of course! And the horse said———"

"What horse? It was a wolf."

"So it was. And this is what it said: 'Take the 75 bus, get out at the main square, turn right, and at the first doorway you'll find three steps. Leave the steps where they are, but pick up the dime you'll find lying on them, and buy yourself a packet of chewing gum.'"

"Grandpa, you're terribly bad at telling stories. You get them all wrong. But all the same, I wouldn't mind some chewing gum."

"All right. Here's your dime." And the old man turned back to his newspaper.

Dick Whittington and His Cat

AN ENGLISH FOLK TALE

Dick Whittington was a poor boy who lived in the country. He had no mother or father, and he had no money to buy food. He dreamed about going to London because he had heard that the streets there were paved with gold.

One day a man on a wagon took Dick to London with him, but when Dick got to London, he found no gold streets. He only saw poor and hungry people like himself.

Dick looked for work, and after a time a kind man hired him as a helper to his cook. But the cook was cruel. He beat Dick and made him sleep in an attic full of mice.

One day, when Dick had saved a penny, he bought a cat. He named the cat Tabby. Tabby was very good at catching mice, and soon there were no more mice in the attic.

Dick's master owned many ships. One day he called all of his servants together. He told them that one of his ships was about to sail to a faraway land. There would be many things on the ship to be traded and sold.

"Each of you may send something of your own on the ship," he said. "When it is sold, you may get much gold and silver." Poor Dick had nothing except Tabby, his cat, so he sent that.

After the cat left, Dick became so lonely and unhappy that he decided to run away. He had not gone far when he heard church bells ringing. They seemed to be saying something:

Turn around, Dick Whittington, turn round,
Three times mayor of London Town.

Dick did not know what the bells meant, but he turned around and went back home.

Some weeks later the ship came back. It was filled with sacks of gold and silver and fine things for everyone—but the biggest treasure of all was for Dick.

"How could a little cat be worth so much?" the people asked. Then the captain of the ship told them the story.

He said that in the country of Barbary the king and queen had invited him to dinner in the palace. When the food was brought out, mice ran out from all sides of the room. They seized the food and ran away with it.

The king and queen said this happened all the time. They said they would give half of their treasure to anyone who would help them get rid of the mice.

Then the captain went off to his ship and brought Tabby back. In a few minutes she had killed all of the mice in the room. The king and queen were amazed. They had never seen a cat before, for there were no cats in the kingdom of Barbary. They said that such a wonderful animal was well worth half of the treasure.

And that was how Dick became one of the richest people in London. Dick went to school, and when he grew up, he married his master's daughter. But Dick never forgot that he had once been poor and hungry, and he was good to the people. That is why he was elected mayor of London three times.

Pussy-Cat, Pussy-Cat

MOTHER GOOSE

Pussy-cat, pussy-cat,
   where have you been?
I've been to London
   to visit the queen.
Pussy-cat, pussy-cat,
   what did you there?
I frightened a little mouse
   under her chair.

The Happy Tailor

LEO TOLSTOY

Once upon a time a rich man and a poor tailor lived in the same house. The rich man lived upstairs, and the poor tailor lived downstairs.

The tailor liked to sing when she worked. She sang one song after another. But the rich man liked to sleep a lot, and the singing bothered him.

114

One day the rich man said, "Tailor, I will give you a bag full of money every day if you will stop singing."

"Fine," said the tailor, so the tailor stopped singing and became richer and richer.

But the more money she got from the rich man, the more unhappy she became because she wanted very much to sing again. Finally she brought all of her money back to the rich man. "Here," she said, "take your money. I cannot be happy if I cannot sing."

And so she gave the money back to the rich man and went away singing. She sang, and she sang, and she was happier than ever before.

Wilbur and Orville

B. ADKINS

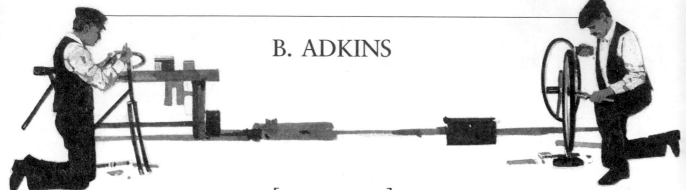

[PART 1]

Wilbur and Orville Wright opened a bicycle shop in 1892. They built and repaired bikes. When they weren't working on bikes, they flew kites or watched birds soaring and gliding in the sky.

"It must be fun to fly," said Orville one day as he watched a bird flying high in the air. "I think about flying a lot. I dream of flying like a bird."

"I do too," said Wilbur. "Some day people will be able to fly. You'll see."

Wilbur and Orville read books by other people who wanted to fly. They studied birds to see why they were able to fly. They made drawings of things that might be able to fly. After reading and studying for quite a while, Orville said, "Let's use one of our drawings to build something that might fly."

Orville and Wilbur worked hard. By 1900 they had made a glider with two wings. It had no engine and would have to glide with the wind.

"Now, let's go to the hill at Kitty Hawk and try to fly," said Wilbur. "The wind is just right today."

The brothers went to Kitty Hawk. First Wilbur took the glider. He ran part of the way down the hill and then jumped up onto the bottom wing. Crash! He didn't fly. Then Orville tried. The same thing happened.

[PART 2]

The Wright brothers decided that they needed to know more about air pressure if they were ever going to fly. They made a six-foot-wide wind tunnel in their bike shop. Then they built and tested two hundred wing models in their tunnel. After two years of testing wings in the wind tunnel, the brothers built a glider that would fly.

"Our glider is very nice, indeed," said Wilbur, "but I'd like to build something that has power."

The Wright brothers built an airplane with a special, lightweight, gasoline engine. They took the airplane to Kitty Hawk to try to fly it. On 17 December 1903 the Wright brothers became the first people to fly an airplane.

Soon the Wright brothers were known all over the world. People in other countries wanted airplanes. The Wright brothers kept working to make their airplanes better and better.

When you look up and see a big, fast, jet airplane in the sky, think about Orville and Wilbur Wright. If the two boys hadn't dreamed of flying many years ago, we might not have such grand airplanes now.

Abu Ali Counts His Donkeys

DOROTHY O. VAN WOERKOM

Abu Ali bought nine donkeys at the fair. He climbed on the first donkey. "Whr-r-r-r!" said Abu Ali. The donkey began to trot, and the other donkeys followed.

"Now," said Abu Ali, "are all my donkeys here?" He turned around and counted. "One—two—three—four—five—six—seven—eight—EIGHT donkeys!"

Abu Ali jumped down from his donkey. He looked behind trees, behind bushes. No donkey. "I will count again," he said. "One—two—three—four—five—six—seven—eight—nine—NINE donkeys!"

Abu Ali climbed back on his donkey. "Whr-r-r-r! Soon I will be home with my nine new donkeys." CLIP, CLAPPETY-CLOP. CLIP, CLAPPETY-CLOP. "Now how many donkeys do I have?" Abu Ali counted EIGHT donkeys!

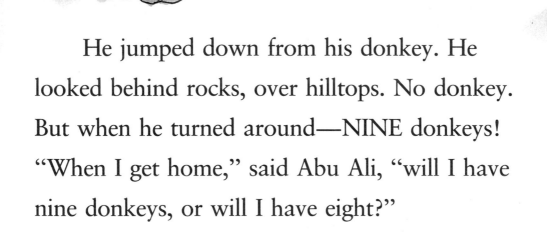

He jumped down from his donkey. He
looked behind rocks, over hilltops. No donkey.
But when he turned around—NINE donkeys!
"When I get home," said Abu Ali, "will I have
nine donkeys, or will I have eight?"

Abu Ali saw his friend Musa coming up the
road. "Help me, friend Musa!" he cried. "I keep
losing a donkey. Now I have nine. But when I
climb on my donkey—like this—I have only eight
donkeys!"

Musa laughed. "Eight donkeys? Nine donkeys? Why, I see TEN donkeys."

"Ten donkeys?" said Abu Ali. "Where do you see ten donkeys?"

"I see eight donkeys following your donkey. I see the donkey you are sitting on." Musa could not stop laughing.

"Oh!" said Abu Ali. "I am sitting on the ninth donkey! But you said you see ten."

"The tenth donkey is the donkey sitting on YOUR donkey," Musa said. "Its name is Abu Ali!"

Clyde Monster

ROBERT L. CROWE

[PART 1]

Clyde wasn't very old, but he was growing—
uglier every day. He lived in a large forest with
his parents.

Father Monster was a big, big monster and
very ugly, which was good. Friends and family
usually make fun of a pretty monster. Mother
Monster was even uglier and greatly admired. All
in all, they were a picture family—as monsters go.

Clyde lived in a cave. That is, he was supposed to live in a cave, at night anyway. During the day, he played in the forest, doing typical monster things like breathing fire at the lake to make the steam rise.

He also did typical Clyde things, like turning somersaults that made large holes in the ground and generally bumping into things. He was more clumsy than the average monster.

At night, Clyde was supposed to go to his cave and sleep. That's when the trouble started. He refused to go to his cave.

"Why?" asked his mother. "Why won't you go to your cave?"

"Because," answered Clyde, "I'm afraid of the dark."

"Afraid!" snorted his father until his nose burned. "A monster of mine afraid? What are you afraid of?"

"People," said Clyde. "I'm afraid there are people in there who will get me."

[PART 2]

"That's silly," said his father. "Come, I'll show you." He breathed a huge burst of fire that lit up the cave. "There. Did you see any people?"

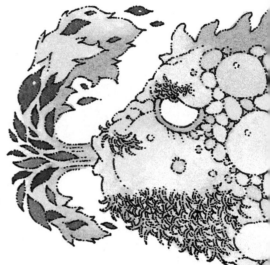

"No," answered Clyde. "But they may be hiding under a rock, and they'll jump out and get me after I'm asleep."

"That is silly," pointed out his mother witl her pointed tongue. "There are no people here. Besides, if there were, they wouldn't hurt you.'

"They wouldn't?" asked Clyde.

"No," said his mother. "Would you ever hide in the dark under a bed or in a closet to scare a human boy or girl?"

129

"Of course not!" exclaimed Clyde, upset that his mother would even think of such a thing.

"Well, people won't hide and scare you either. A long time ago monsters and people made a deal," explained his father. "Monsters don't scare people—and people don't scare monsters."

"Are you sure?" Clyde asked.

"Absolutely," said his mother. "Do you know of a monster who was ever frightened by a people?

"No," answered Clyde after some thought.

"Do you know of any boys or girls who were ever frightened by a monster?

"No," he answered quickly.

"There!" said his mother. "Now off to bed."

"And no more nonsense about being scared by people," ordered his father.

"Okay," said Clyde, as he stumbled into the cave. "But, could you leave the rock open just a little?"

Glossary

Pronunciation Key

a_, ă_	apple, tan		g	gas, wiggle, sag
ā	acorn, table		ġ	gem, giant, gym
à	alone, Donna		gh_	ghost
â	air, care		_gh	though, thought (silent)
ä	father, wand		h_	hat
a̱	all, ball		i_, ĭ_	it, sit
a_e	ape, bake		ī	pilot, pie
ai_	aim, sail		_ï_	babies, machine, *also*
àr	calendar			onion, savior, familiar
är	art, park, car		i_e	ice, bite
au_	author, Paul		_igh	high, bright
aw	awful, lawn, saw		ir	irk, bird, fir
_ay	say, day		j_	jam
b	bat, able, tub		k	kite, ankle, ink
c	cat, cot, cut		kn_	knife
ce	cent, ace		l	lamp, wallet, tail
ch	chest, church		_le	table, ample
c̄h	chorus, ache		m	man, bump, ham
c̆h	chute		_mb	lamb, comb
ci	cider, decide		n	no, tent, sun
_ci_	special		_ñ_	uncle, anger
_ck	tack, sick		_ng	sing, ring
cy	bicycle		o_, ŏ_	odd, pot
d	dad		ō	go, no, toe
_dge	edge, judge		ȯ	come, wagon
e_, ě_	elf, hen		ô	off, song
ē	equal, me		oa_	oat, soap
ė	moment, loaded		o_e	ode, bone
ea	eat, leap, tea		oi_	oil, boil
_ĕa_	head, bread		ŏo	book, nook
ee	eel, feet, see		o̅o̅	boot, zoo
er	herd, her		or	order, normal
_ew	few, blew		ȯr	motor, doctor
f	far, taffy, off		ou_	out, hound

ow	owl, town, cow	ṻ	truth, true
_ōw	low, throw	u̇	nature
_oy	boy, toy	u̲	pull, full
p	paper, tap	ur	urge, turn, fur
ph	phone, elephant, graph	ūr	cure, pure
qu_	quick, queen	v	voice, save
r	ram, born, ear	w_	will, wash
s	sun, ask, yes	wh_	white, what
_s̲	toes, hose	wr_	write
_s̲_	vision, confusion	_x	extra, ax
ss̲	fission	_x̲_	exist, example
sh	show, bishop, fish	y_	yes, yet
t	tall, sets, bit	_y	baby, happy (when
th	thick, three		it is the only
t̲h	this, feather, bathe		vowel in a final
_tch	itch, patch		unstressed
_t̲i_	nation, station,		syllable)
	also question	_y̆_	cymbal
t̲u	congratulate	_ȳ	cry, sky
u_, ŭ_	up, bus	ẏ	zephyr, martyr
ū	use, cute, *also* granulate	z	zoo, nozzle, buzz

1. If a word ends in a silent *e*, as in **face**, the silent *e* is not marked. If a word ends in *-ed* pronounced **t**, as in **baked**, or **d**, as in **stayed**, no mark is needed. If the ending *-ed* forms a separate syllable pronounced ėd, as in **load'ėd**, the *e* has a dot.

2. If there are two or three vowels in the same syllable and only one is marked, as in **beaū'ty, friĕnd, rōgue,** or **breāk,** all the other vowels in the syllable are silent.

3. The Open Court diacritical marks in the Pronunciation Key make it possible to indicate the pronunciation of most unfamiliar words without respelling.

ab•sò•lūte′ly *adv.* without any doubt; for certain

Ä′bū̱ Ä′li

ac′cĭ•dèn′tàl•ly *adv.* not done on purpose; not meant to happen

ad•mire′ *v.* to be pleased with

Af′ri•cà *n.* one of the continents, or large areas of land on Earth

à•mazed′ *v.* surprised

är′ti•cle *n.* a written report that is published in a newspaper or magazine

at′tic *n.* the top floor of a house, usually small and used to store things

av′er•aġe *adj.* ordinary; usual

bat′ter•y *n.* a container of chemicals that works to make electricity

bė•have′ *v.* to act in a certain way

bė•hāv′ïòr *n.* a way of acting

bound *v.* to leap with long steps while running

burst *n.* a small, quick explosion

chim•pan•zee′ *n.* a kind of ape

clum′sy *adj.* often bumping into things or knocking things over

Clȳde Mon′ster

cob′webs *n.* old, dusty spider webs

creak *v.* to make a squeaking noise

crūde *adj.* not perfect

crū'ėl *adj.* mean or hurtful

crum'pled *adj.* wrinkled or crushed

dâre *v.* to try something dangerous or difficult

dè•nȳ' *v.* to keep something from someone

Dick Whit'ting•tòn

dis•còv'er•y *n.* something new that is found out

dis'tànce *n.* the amount of space from one place to another place

dor'mouse *n.* a small animal that looks like a furry squirrel and sleeps a lot

Dr. Loū'is Leak'ēy

ech'ō *v.* to copy or repeat a sound

E•len'ä

fan•tas'tic *adj.* so wonderful that it is hard to believe

for•lorn' *adj.* sad; lonely

Pronunciation Key

VOWELS: sat, hăve, āble, fäther, ạll, câre, àlone; yet, brĕad, mē, loadėd; it, practĭce, pīlot, machĭne; hot, nō, ôff, wagòn; foŏt, fōod; oil, toy; count, town; up, ūse, trụth, pụll; mȳth, baby, crȳ, zephȳr.

CONSONANTS: cent, cider, cycle; c̄horus, c̲hute; ġem; light, and though (silent), ghost; iñk, elephant; toeṣ; t̲hem; speçial, meaṣure, natįon, natụre.

ġin′ġer•brĕad *n.* a dark cookie or cake made with a spice called ginger

glide *v.* to fly smoothly and gently

glīd′er *n.* a small, light airplane that has no engine but uses the air to fly

gnaw (naw) *v.* to chew on something with sharp teeth

gob′lin *n.* a very tiny, make-believe person who often gets into trouble

Gōld′ĭ•locks

Gō′mėz

grand *adj.* large and wonderful

hâre *n.* a gray or brown animal that looks like a large rabbit

haul *v.* to carry a heavy load from one place to another

heap *n.* a high, round pile

his′tȯ•ry *n.* what has happened in the past

hoist *v.* to lift high in the air

hol′lōw *adj.* empty

in•vent′ *v.* to make or do something for the first time

Jane Gōōd′all

Johnny (Jon′ny)

Kit′ty Hawk

là•ment′ *v.* to complain sadly

lest *conj.* in order not to

lī′cėnse *n.* a card that says you are allowed to do
    something

limb *n.* a branch from a tree

Lȯn′dôn *n.* a city in England

mạlt *n.* grain soaked in water until it tastes sweet

mär′kėt *n.* an outdoor store

min′nōw *n.* a tiny fish

Miss Fin′nēy

mod′ėl *n.* something that is built to test a new idea

moist *adj.* a little wet; damp

Mrs. Ben′jà•min

Mū′sä

nō′tiȯn *n.* an idea

Pronunciation Key

VOWELS: sat, hăve, āble, fäther, ạll, câre, àlone; yet, brĕad, mē, loadėd; it, practĭce,
pīlot, machǐne; hot, nō, ôff, wagȯn; fŏŏt, fōōd; oil, toy; count, town; up, ūse, trụth,
pụll; mў̆th, baby, crȳ, zephȳr.

CONSONANTS: cent, cider, cycle; c̄horus, c̲hute; ġem; light, and though (silent), ghost;
iñk, elephant; toeṣ; t̲hem; speçial, meaṣure, naṭion, naṭure.

Ôf′fi•cer Cär•mel′lä

Paul′à

pave *v.* to make a street or road

Pe′drō

pen *n.* an area of land with a fence around it for keeping
    animals in

phōn′y *adj.* fake; not real

plain *n.* a large area of flat country

plod *v.* to walk slowly and heavily

plum *n.* a small, sweet, purple fruit

pōk′er *n.* a long, metal rod used for stirring up a fire

por′ridge *n.* cereal cooked in water or milk

pow′er *v.* to run

pow′er *n.* strength; energy

proj′ect *n.* a big job

rap *v.* to knock loudly

rē•chärġe′ *v.* to give more energy to

rė•pâir′ *v.* to fix something that is broken

Rï•cär′dō

rich *adj.* having many good things in it

rubbed *v.* shined; polished

sau′cer *n.* a small, round plate placed under a cup

scī′ėn•tist *n.* a person who studies nature

scour *v.* to scrub until clean

sēize *v.* to grab and run away with

serv′ȧnt *n.* a person paid to help take care of a house

shep•herd (shep′erd) *n.* a person who takes care of sheep and keeps them from danger

shore *n.* the edge of the land next to the water

side′track *n.* a small railroad track that leads off the main track

sight *n.* an interesting thing to see

silk′worm *n.* a worm that spins a wrapping from which silk is made

siñk *v.* to fall

soar *v.* to fly upward

sȯm′er•sault *v.* to roll on the head and hands in a circle; to roll head over heels

stȯm′aċh *n.* the part of the body to which food goes after it is eaten

---

Pronunciation Key

VOWELS: sat, hăve, able, fäther, all, câre, ȧlone; yet, brĕad, mē, loadėd; it, practĭce, pīlot, machīne; hot, nō, ȯff, wagȯn; fŏŏt, fōōd; oil, toy; count, town; up, ūse, trṳth, pṳll; mўth, baby, crў, zephўr.

CONSONANTS: cent, cider, cycle; ċhorus, ċhute; ġem; light, and though (silent), **gh**ost; iñk, elephant; toe**s**; **th**em; special, mea**s**ure, na**t**ion, na**t**ure.

stud′y *v.* to learn about

sub′sti•tūte *n.* something or someone used in place of another

tai′lȯr *n.* a person whose job is to sew clothes

tat′tėrėd *adj.* worn; ragged

tend *v.* to take care of; to watch over

tide *v.* to help or hold

toad′sto͞ol *n.* a large mushroom

tor′tȯise *n.* a large turtle

tramp *v.* to walk heavily and noisily

trĕaş′ure *n.* money, gold, jewels, and other valuable things that have been saved by someone

trem′ble *v.* to shake with fear

trōll *n.* an ugly, make-believe creature in some folk tales

trō′phy *n.* a reward, usually a small statue, given to a winner

trust *v.* to be sure that someone will not cause hurt; to believe in someone

twiñk′ling *n.* a very short time; a moment

tўp′i•cȧl *adj.* usual

Wil′bur and Ôr′ville Wright

Wil′lȧ•by

wȯrth *adj.* deserving of

wȯrth′lėss *adj.* of no use